AMANPREET KAUR

Smart Money Saving Tips for Financial Success

First published by Rana Books UK 2023

Copyright © 2023 by Amanpreet Kaur

All rights reserved. No part of this publication may be reproduced, stored or transmitted in any form or by any means, electronic, mechanical, photocopying, recording, scanning, or otherwise without written permission from the publisher. It is illegal to copy this book, post it to a website, or distribute it by any other means without permission.

Register Publisher: RANA BOOKS INDIA

VPO RALLA,MANSA 151510, PB, INDIA

First edition

Contents

1. Introduction — 1
2. Setting Financial Goals — 8
3. Budgeting Strategies — 11
4. Saving on Everyday Expenses — 16
5. Strategies for Saving on Housing — 21
6. Saving for Retirement — 28
7. Paying Off Debt — 33
8. Income-Boosting Strategies — 39
9. Smart Shopping Techniques — 44
10. Long-Term Financial Planning — 48
11. Money Saving Tips — 53

1

Introduction

1. Introduction

Saving money is an essential skill that everyone should develop. It provides financial security flexibility and the opportunity to achieve your long-term goals. In this book we will explore various money-saving tips that can help you build a solid financial foundation.

1.1 Importance of Saving Money

Saving money is important for several reasons:

a) Emergency Fund: Life is unpredictable and unexpected expenses can arise at any time. Having a sufficient emergency fund ensures that you are prepared to handle any unforeseen circumstances such as medical emergencies car repairs or job loss.

b) Financial Independence: Saving money gives you the freedom to make independent financial decisions. It allows you to be less dependent on loans and credit reducing stress and increasing peace of mind.

c) Achieving Dreams and Goals: Whether it's buying a house starting a business or traveling the world saving money is crucial for achieving your long-term goals. It helps you accumulate the necessary funds to turn your dreams into reality.

1.2 Benefits of Saving Money

Saving money provides numerous benefits that go beyond financial security:

a) Financial Freedom: Saving money gives you the freedom to enjoy life without the constant stress of living paycheck to paycheck. It allows you to have more control over your financial choices allowing you to focus on what truly matters to you.

b) Reduced Stress: Financial stress is a common problem for many individuals. Having savings in place relieves financial pressure lowers stress levels and improves overall well-being.

c) Investment Opportunities: Saving money provides you with the opportunity to invest and grow your wealth. Investing in stocks real estate or other assets can generate passive income and increase your net worth over time.

Now that we understand the importance and benefits of saving money let's explore some practical tips and strategies to help you save effectively.

2. Budgeting and Tracking Expenses

The first step in saving money is creating a budget and tracking your expenses. Budgeting allows you to allocate your income towards various categories such as housing transportation groceries and entertainment. By knowing where your money is going you can identify areas where you can cut back and save.

- Example: Suppose your monthly income is $4000. After deducting essential expenses like rent ($1200 utilities ($200 and groceries ($400 you have $2200 left. By tracking your expenses you realize you spend $300 on dining out and $200 on entertainment. By reducing these discretionary expenses you can potentially save an additional $500 each month.

3. Cut Back on Unnecessary Expenses

Identifying and eliminating unnecessary expenses is a powerful way to save money. Many of our everyday spending habits are non-essential and can be easily cut back or eliminated. Here are a few ways to achieve this:

a) Meal Planning and Cooking at Home: Eating out can be expensive. Planning your meals in advance cooking at home and bringing lunch to work can save you a significant amount of money.

b) Cancel Subscriptions and Memberships: Review your subscriptions and cancel those that you don't use regularly. This includes gym memberships streaming services or magazine subscriptions that you rarely utilize.

c) Negotiate Bills and Expenses: Contact your service providers (internet cable insurance) and negotiate lower rates. Many companies are willing to offer discounts if you're a loyal customer or if you mention better deals from their competitors.

- Example: By cutting back on dining out and canceling unused subscriptions you can save an extra $200 per month.

4. Automate Savings

Automating savings is an effective strategy to ensure consistent and disciplined saving. By setting up automatic transfers to a savings account you eliminate the temptation to spend the money.

- Example: Set up an automatic transfer of $200 from your checking account to your savings account every payday. This ensures that you save $400 per month without any effort helping you reach your financial goals faster.

5. Comparison Shopping

Before making any major purchases it's important to do thorough research and compare prices. With the abundance of online shopping platforms and tools it's easier than ever to find the best deals.

- Example: If you're in the market for a new laptop research different brands and compare prices across various websites. You may find the same product at a significantly lower price by taking the time to compare.

6. Use Coupons Rewards and Cashback Offers

Taking advantage of coupons rewards programs and cashback offers can help you save money on your everyday purchases. Many retailers and credit card companies offer cashback incentives or loyalty points that can be redeemed for discounts or future purchases.

- Example: If you regularly shop at a specific grocery store sign up for their rewards program. By accumulating points you can earn discounts or free products ultimately reducing your overall grocery expenses.

7. Energy Efficiency

Reducing your energy consumption not only helps the environment but also saves you money on utility bills. Implementing energy-efficient practices within your home can significantly lower your monthly expenses.

- Example: Switching to energy-efficient light bulbs installing programmable thermostats and unplugging unused electronics can save you hundreds of dollars annually.

8. Explore Alternative Transportation Options

Transportation costs can quickly add up especially if you rely heavily on your car. Exploring alternative transportation options can save you money on fuel parking and maintenance.

- Example: Consider carpooling biking or using public transportation as alternatives to driving alone. By reducing your dependence on your car you can save a substantial amount of money each month.

9. DIY Projects and Repairs

Instead of hiring professionals for every home improvement or repair task consider tackling some DIY projects yourself. Learning basic repair skills can save you money on labor costs.

- Example: Suppose your faucet is leaking. Instead of calling a plumber watch a tutorial video and fix it yourself. You can save anywhere from $100 to $200 on labor expenses.

10. Set Realistic Goals and Reward Yourself

When setting savings goals it's important to be realistic and achievable. Set milestones along the way and reward yourself for reaching them. Celebrating your achievements keeps you motivated and makes the process more enjoyable.

- Example: If your goal is to save $10000 in a year break it down into smaller monthly or quarterly targets. For every milestone achieved treat yourself to a small reward such as a nice dinner or a movie night.

Conclusion

Saving money is a lifelong journey that requires perseverance and discipline. By implementing these money-saving tips and strategies you can take control of your finances achieve your goals and build a secure future. Remember every small step towards saving adds up to significant progress over time.

2

Setting Financial Goals

Setting financial goals is an important aspect of money saving. It involves determining the objectives you want to achieve with your money. By setting clear goals you not only have a clear vision of what you want to achieve but you also have a roadmap to guide your financial decisions.

2.1 Identifying Short-term and Long-term Goals

When setting financial goals it's important to distinguish between short-term and long-term goals. Short-term goals are those that can be accomplished within a relatively short period of time usually within a year or less. Examples of short-term goals include paying off a credit card debt saving up for a vacation or buying a new gadget.

Long-term goals are those that take longer to achieve often spanning several years or even decades. Examples of long-term goals include saving for retirement buying a house or funding your child's education.

It's important to identify both short-term and long-term goals because they require different strategies and approaches. Short-term goals usually require a smaller amount of money but they may require more immediate action and discipline. Long-term goals on the other hand require consistent saving and long-term planning.

2.2 Prioritizing Goals based on Importance and Urgency

Once you have identified your financial goals it's essential to prioritize them based on their importance and urgency. Prioritizing helps you allocate your resources effectively ensuring that you focus on the goals that are most important to you.

To prioritize your goals start by assessing the level of urgency for each goal. Some goals may have more immediate deadlines such as paying off high-interest debt or funding a medical emergency. These goals should be given higher priority since they require immediate action.

Next consider the importance of each goal to you personally. Everyone has different priorities so it's crucial to identify which goals hold the most significance in your life. For example if you value financial security saving for retirement may be a higher priority for you than buying a luxury car.

Once you have assessed the urgency and importance of each goal you can create a prioritized list. This list helps you stay focused and make informed decisions about how to allocate your income and resources.

For example let's say you have identified the following financial goals:
1. Paying off credit card debt ($5000)
2. Saving for a vacation ($2000)
3. Funding an emergency fund ($10000)
4. Saving for a down payment on a house ($50000)
5. Saving for retirement ($500000)

Based on urgency paying off credit card debt should be given the highest priority since it may incur high interest rates. Funding an emergency fund should be the next priority to ensure financial security during unexpected events. Saving for retirement could be given a lower priority since it is a long-term goal that requires consistent saving over time.

By prioritizing your goals you can allocate your income accordingly. For example you may decide to allocate a portion of your monthly income towards paying off credit card debt while also setting aside a specific amount for the vacation fund. This way you are actively working towards your goals and managing your finances efficiently.

In conclusion setting financial goals is an essential step towards effective money saving. By identifying both short-term and long-term goals and prioritizing them based on importance and urgency you can create a roadmap to achieve financial success. Remember goal setting is a dynamic process and it's important to regularly reassess and adjust your goals as your financial situation evolves.

3

Budgeting Strategies

3.1 Creating an Effective Budget:

Creating a budget is the foundation of any successful money-saving plan. It helps you gain control over your finances allocate your income wisely and plan for the future. Here are some steps to create an effective budget:

a) Calculate your income: Start by determining your total monthly income. Include all sources such as your salary investments and any other income streams.

b) List your fixed expenses: Fixed expenses include essential costs that remain relatively constant each month such as rent or mortgage payments loan repayments insurance premiums and utility bills. Write down these expenses and their respective amounts.

c) Identify your flexible expenses: Flexible expenses are variable costs that can be adjusted based on your priorities. This category may include groceries dining out entertainment transportation and personal care expenses. Estimate the amount you typically spend on each expense and allocate it accordingly.

d) Set financial goals: Determine your short-term and long-term financial goals such as saving for emergencies paying off debts or saving for a vacation. Allocate a portion of your income towards these goals.

e) Determine your savings rate: Subtract your total expenses (fixed and flexible) and financial goals from your income. The remaining amount is what you can save each month. Aim to save at least 20% of your income but adjust it based on your individual circumstances.

3.2 Tracking Expenses and Income:

One of the key aspects of effective budgeting is tracking your expenses and income. This allows you to identify areas where you can cut back and make adjustments. Here are some methods to track your finances:

a) Use a budgeting app: There are numerous budgeting apps available that can automatically track your expenses and income. These apps categorize your spending provide visual representations of your financial data and offer insights into your overall financial health.

b) Maintain a spending journal: If you prefer a more hands-on approach you can keep a spending journal where you manually record your expenses and income. This gives you a clearer picture of where your money is going and helps you identify any patterns or areas of overspending.

c) Review bank and credit card statements: Regularly review your bank and credit card statements to track your expenses. Look for any recurring charges unnecessary subscriptions or error that you can rectify. This helps you stay on top of your finances and identify places to cut expenses.

3.3 Cutting unnecessary expenses:

Reducing unnecessary expenses is a significant way to free up money to save. Here are some effective strategies to cut back on expenses:

a) Eliminate discretionary spending: Identify non-essential expenses and cut back or eliminate them. This could include dining out buying expensive coffee unnecessary shopping or entertainment subscriptions that you rarely use.

b) Negotiate bills and subscriptions: Contact your service providers to negotiate better rates for utilities cable TV internet or insurance plans. Additionally review your subscriptions such as gym memberships or streaming services and cancel those you don't frequently use.

c) Reduce food costs: Plan your meals in advance make a grocery list and stick to it. Avoid impulse purchases and use coupons or store discounts whenever possible. Consider cooking at home more often as it is generally cheaper than eating out.

d) Smart shopping: Before making a purchase compare prices read reviews and look for discounts or promotional offers. Purchase items in bulk or wait for sales to get the best deals.

e) Save on transportation: Consider carpooling or using public transportation to reduce fuel and parking costs. If feasible consider biking or walking for short distances instead of relying on vehicles.

3.4 Implementing the 50/30/20 Rule for Budgeting:

The 50/30/20 rule is a popular budgeting strategy that helps allocate your income effectively. Here's how it works:

a) 50% for essentials: Allocate 50% of your income towards essential expenses such as housing utilities transportation groceries and healthcare. These are the necessities that you need to sustain your daily life.

b) 30% for discretionary spending: Allocate 30% of your income towards discretionary spending which includes entertainment dining out non-essential shopping and hobbies. This portion allows you to enjoy life and have some flexibility in your budget.

c) 20% for savings and debt repayment: Dedicate 20% of your income towards savings and debt repayment. This includes building an emergency fund saving for retirement paying off debts and investing. This portion ensures you're working towards your long-term financial goals.

By implementing the 50/30/20 rule you can achieve a balance between enjoying your money now and planning for a secure financial future.

In conclusion budgeting strategies such as creating an effective budget tracking expenses and income cutting unnecessary expenses and implementing the 50/30/20 rule can help you save money. By analyzing your income expenses and financial goals you can make informed decisions about where to allocate your money reduce unnecessary spending and increase your savings rate. Ultimately budgeting is a powerful tool that can bring financial stability and help you achieve your money-saving objectives.

4

Saving on Everyday Expenses

4.1 Tips for Saving on Food and Groceries:

4.1.1 Meal Planning and Bulk Buying: One of the most effective ways to save money on food is by meal planning and buying items in bulk. By planning your meals ahead of time you can create a grocery list with only the necessary ingredients avoiding last-minute impulse buys. Additionally buying in bulk can be cost-effective especially for staple items like rice pasta and canned goods.

4.1.2 Couponing and Discount Apps: Coupons and discount apps are valuable tools for saving money on groceries. Look for coupons in newspapers magazines and online platforms. There are also various smartphone apps that offer digital coupons price comparison features and cashback options.

4.1.3 Buy Generic Brands: Consider buying generic or store brands instead of name brands. The quality is often similar but the price difference can be significant. Compare prices and ingredients to make an informed decision.

4.1.4 Cook at Home: Eating out in restaurants or ordering takeout can be quite expensive. By cooking at home you can save a significant amount of money. Try to prepare larger portions and freeze leftovers for future meals. This way you can also save time on busy days.

4.1.5 Grow Your Own Food: If you have the space and time consider creating a vegetable garden or growing some herbs indoors. This can be a fun and rewarding way to save money on groceries as well as enjoy fresh and organic produce.

4.2 Strategies for Saving on Utilities:

4.2.1 Energy Conservation: Adopt energy-saving habits such as turning off lights when not in use using energy-efficient appliances and maximizing natural light during the day. Additionally adjust your thermostat to a reasonable temperature to reduce heating and cooling costs.

4.2.2 Water Conservation: Be mindful of water usage by fixing leaks taking shorter showers and using water-saving devices such as low-flow showerheads and dual-flush toilets. Also consider collecting rainwater for watering plants and gardens.

4.2.3 Unplug Electronics: Even when turned off electronics can still consume energy if they are plugged in. To avoid this "vampire power" usage unplug devices or use power strips that can be easily switched off when not in use.

4.2.4 Use Energy-Saving Bulbs: Replace traditional incandescent light bulbs with energy-saving ones like LED or CFL bulbs. Although they may have a higher upfront cost they last longer and consume significantly less energy.

4.2.5 Compare and Switch Providers: Take the time to compare utility providers and their rates to ensure you are getting the best deal. Consider switching providers if you find a better offer but make sure to consider any termination fees or contract obligations.

4.3 Cutting Costs on Transportation:
   4.3.1 Carpooling and Public Transportation: Whenever possible consider carpooling with friends neighbors or colleagues for commuting or running errands. Public transportation options such as buses trains or trams can also be more cost-effective than driving alone.

4.3.2 Fuel Efficiency: Practicing fuel-efficient driving techniques such as maintaining proper tire pressure reducing excessive idling and avoiding rapid acceleration and heavy braking can help save money on fuel costs.

4.3.3 Bike or Walk: If the distance allows opt for walking or biking instead of driving. Not only will this save on transportation costs but it also has health and environmental benefits.

4.3.4 Maintenance and Repair: Regular vehicle maintenance such as tune-ups oil changes and tire rotations can prevent costly repairs in the future. Paying attention to small issues and addressing them promptly can save you money in the long run.

4.3.5 Car Insurance Comparison: Periodically review your car insurance policy and compare rates from different providers.

You might be able to find more affordable coverage without compromising on quality.

4.4 Reducing Entertainment Expenses:

4.4.1 Streaming Services: Consider reducing the number of streaming services you subscribe to. Evaluate your usage and select the most essential ones or share subscriptions with family or friends to split costs.

4.4.2 Library and Secondhand Books: Instead of buying new books explore the offerings at your local library or shop at secondhand bookstores. You can borrow books for free or purchase them at discounted prices.

4.4.3 Free or Low-Cost Activities: Look for free or low-cost entertainment options such as community events park outings museums with free entry days or outdoor concerts. Take advantage of public resources available in your area.

4.4.4 DIY Projects and Hobbies: Engaging in do-it-yourself (DIY) projects and hobbies can be both enjoyable and cost-effective. Consider activities like gardening painting knitting or woodworking. These hobbies can also provide you with unique gifts or items for personal use.

4.4.5 Negotiate Bills and Memberships: Review your monthly subscriptions and membership fees. Consider contacting service providers to negotiate lower rates or look for alternative options if necessary.

By implementing these money-saving tips in various aspects

of your everyday life you can effectively reduce your expenses and increase your savings. Remember every small change adds up and over time you can build a solid financial foundation for a better future.

5

Strategies for Saving on Housing

5.1 Renting vs. Buying: Pros and Cons

When it comes to housing one of the first decisions you need to make is whether to rent or buy. Each option has its own advantages and disadvantages so it's essential to consider your individual circumstances before making a decision.

Renting Pros:
 - Flexibility: Renting offers more flexibility as it allows you to easily move to upfront costs: Renting typically requires a smaller upfront cost compared to buying a home as you only need to provide a security deposit and possibly the first month's rent.
 - Limited responsibility: As a renter you are not responsible for property maintenance or repairs. These responsibilities fall on the landlord saving you time and money.
 - Access to amenities: Many rental properties come with amenities such as gym facilities pools or maintenance services that may be costly if you own a home.

Renting Cons:

- Lack of equity: Monthly rent payments do not build equity meaning you do not gain ownership in the property over time.

- No control over the property: Renters are subject to the landlord's rules and policies limiting your ability to make changes or improvements to the property.

- Rent increases: Landlords may increase the rent over time potentially making your monthly housing costs less predictable.

- Limited customization: Renting often restricts your ability to customize or personalize the space to your liking.

Buying Pros:

- Investment opportunity: Purchasing a home allows you to build equity which can be a valuable asset over time. You have the potential to sell the property for a profit or use it as an investment.

- Stability: Owning a home provides stability giving you the freedom to stay in one place without worrying about lease agreements or potential evictions.

- Tax benefits: Homeowners can benefit from tax deductions on mortgage interest and property taxes which can save you money.

- Customization: When you own a property you have the freedom to make changes and renovations to create the home of your dreams.

Buying Cons:

- Higher upfront costs: Buying a home generally requires a significant upfront investment including a down payment closing costs and other associated fees.

- Responsibility for maintenance: Homeowners are responsible for maintenance and repairs which can be costly and time-consuming.

- Limited flexibility: Owning a home ties you to a specific location which can limit your ability to move or take advantage of job opportunities in other areas.

- Market volatility: Real estate markets can fluctuate and if property values decline you may face difficulties in selling your home or refinancing your mortgage.

5.2 Negotiating Rental or Mortgage Terms

If you decide to rent or buy a property there are strategies you can use to negotiate better rental or mortgage terms helping you save money in the long run.

Rent Negotiation Tips:

- Research the market: Before negotiating your rent research rental prices in the area to determine if you're paying a fair amount. Websites and apps can provide insights into the current market rates.

- Highlight your strengths: If you have a stable income good credit score or can provide references use these to your advantage during negotiations. Landlords may be willing to lower the rent or offer other concessions if they perceive you as a responsible tenant.

- Lease term flexibility: Negotiate the terms of your lease such as the length of the lease or the possibility of a rent freeze for a certain period. Longer lease terms or signing a lease during a slower rental season may give you more negotiating power.

- Offer prepayment or longer advance notice: Offering to prepay rent or provide longer advance notice for moving out can be appealing to landlords as it reduces their perceived risk. In return they may be willing to lower your monthly rent.

- Ask for upgrades or repairs: If the property requires repairs or upgrades negotiate with the landlord to either lower the rent or cover the costs of the improvements.

Mortgage Negotiation Tips:

- Compare lenders: Shop around for mortgages and compare offers from different lenders. This allows you to negotiate better terms including interest rates loan fees and repayment options.

- Improve credit score: A higher credit score can make you eligible for better mortgage terms. Pay off debts reduce credit utilization and correct any errors on your credit report to improve your score before applying for a mortgage.

- Consider a larger down payment: Making a larger down payment (if financially feasible) can lower your mortgage rates or eliminate the need for private mortgage insurance (PMI saving you money over the life of the loan.

- Use a mortgage broker: Mortgage brokers have access to multiple lenders and can negotiate on your behalf to find the best mortgage deal. They may have access to exclusive rates or deals that are not publicly available.

- Negotiate mortgage terms and fees: Discuss potential options with your lender including negotiating the interest rate loan origination fees and closing costs. Being well-informed and willing to negotiate can save you thousands of dollars over the life of your mortgage.

5.3 Ways to Lower Homeowners Insurance Costs

Homeowners insurance is an essential expense to protect your property and belongings from unforeseen events. However there are strategies to reduce the cost of homeowners insurance without compromising coverage.

- Shop around: Obtain quotes from multiple insurance providers to compare prices and coverage options. Different insurance companies may offer varying rates so taking the time to research and compare can result in significant savings.

- Opt for a higher deductible: Increasing your deductible which is the amount you pay before insurance coverage kicks in can lower your monthly premiums. However be sure to choose a deductible that you can afford to pay in case of a claim.

- Bundle insurance policies: Many insurance companies offer discounts if you bundle multiple policies such as homeowners and auto insurance with the same provider. Ask your insurance provider if this option is available.

- Improve home security: Installing security systems smoke detectors fire alarms and other safety features can lead to discounts on homeowners insurance premiums. These measures reduce the risk of theft fire or other potential damages.

- Maintain a good credit score: Insurance providers often consider credit history when determining premiums. Maintaining a good credit score can help you secure lower insurance rates.

- Review coverage limits: Regularly assess your insurance coverage to ensure it accurately reflects the value of your property and possessions. Over-insuring can result in unnecessary expenses while under-insuring can leave you vulnerable in case of a claim.

- Stay loyal to your insurer: Loyalty can be rewarded by insurance companies. Some insurers offer discounts to long-term customers so it's worth inquiring about potential savings if you've been with the same provider for an extended period.

5.4 Reducing Energy Consumption in the Home

Energy consumption in the home can be a significant expense but there are various strategies you can use to reduce energy consumption conserving resources and saving money.

- Upgrade to energy-efficient appliances: Replace old energy-intensive appliances with more energy-efficient models. Look for appliances with an ENERGY STAR label as they meet strict energy efficiency standards. Upgrading to energy-efficient appliances can significantly reduce your energy consumption and lower your utility bills over time.
- Use programmable thermostats: Programmable thermostats allow you to set temperature schedules and automatically adjust HVAC (heating ventilation and air conditioning) settings. By optimizing temperature control when you're at home or away you can reduce energy waste and save on heating and cooling costs.
- Install energy-efficient lighting: Replace traditional incandescent light bulbs with energy-efficient alternatives such as LED or CFL bulbs. These bulbs consume significantly less energy and have a longer lifespan.
- Improve insulation and weatherproofing: Proper insulation and weatherproofing can prevent heat loss or gain reducing the need for excess heating or cooling. Sealing gaps and adding insulation to windows doors and attics can result in substantial energy savings.
- Unplug idle electronics: Many electronics consume energy even when they're turned off or in standby mode. Unplug devices

when they're not in use or use power strips with switches to easily turn off multiple devices at once.

- Adjust water heater settings: Lower the temperature of your water heater to a comfortable but energy-efficient level. Heating water requires a significant amount of energy so reducing the temperature can lead to noticeable savings on energy bills.

- Maximize natural lighting: Make the most of natural lighting during the day by opening curtains or blinds. This reduces the need for artificial lighting and saves electricity.

- Use energy-efficient window coverings: Install blinds or curtains designed to insulate your windows reducing heat transfer in hot weather and retaining heat during colder months.

- Regular HVAC maintenance: Schedule regular maintenance for your heating and cooling systems to ensure they operate efficiently. Clean or replace air filters regularly and have a professional service your HVAC system to maintain optimal energy performance.

By implementing these strategies you can save money on housing-related expenses whether you choose to rent or buy. From negotiating rental or mortgage terms to reducing homeowners insurance costs and minimizing energy consumption these tips can help you achieve financial stability and long-term savings. Remember to assess your unique circumstances and make decisions that align with your goals and financial situation.

6

Saving for Retirement

6.1 Understanding Retirement Accounts and Options:

Saving for retirement is a crucial aspect of financial planning. One of the most effective ways to save for retirement is through retirement accounts. Understanding the different types of retirement accounts and options available is essential in making informed decisions about your savings strategies. Here are some key retirement accounts and options:

1. 401(k) Plans: Many employers offer 401(k) plans as a benefit to their employees. These plans allow you to contribute a portion of your salary to your retirement savings on a pre-tax basis. The contributions are often matched by your employer which is essentially free money. The funds grow tax-free until you withdraw them in retirement.

Example: Let's say you earn $50000 per year and contribute 5% of your salary to your 401(k) plan. That would be $2500 per year. If your employer matches your contributions up to 50 they would add an extra $1250 to your account annually.

2. Individual Retirement Accounts (IRAs): IRAs are retirement accounts that individuals can open on their own. There are two main types of IRAs - Traditional and Roth. Traditional IRAs allow you to contribute pre-tax income and the withdrawals are taxable in retirement. Roth IRAs on the other hand use after-tax income for contributions and qualified withdrawals are tax-free.

Example: If you contribute $6000 per year to a Traditional IRA for 30 years and your tax rate at retirement is 20 you would have saved $180000 in pre-tax dollars. In retirement if you withdraw $10000 per year you would pay $2000 in taxes annually.

3. Pension Plans: Some individuals are fortunate enough to have pension plans offered by their employers. These plans provide a guaranteed income stream in retirement based on your years of service and salary history.

Example: If you work for a company for 30 years and your pension plan provides 2% of your average salary for each year of service and your average salary is $60000 you would receive $36000 per year in retirement.

6.2 Tips for Maximizing Contributions to Retirement Funds:

Once you understand the different retirement account options available it's important to take steps to maximize your contributions. Here are some tips to help you save more for retirement:

1. Set Clear Goals: Determine how much money you will need in

retirement taking into account factors such as inflation lifestyle expectations and healthcare costs. Having a clear goal will motivate you to save more.

2. Automate Contributions: Set up automatic transfers from your paycheck to your retirement accounts. By doing this your contributions become consistent and regular helping you stay on track with your savings goals.

3. Take Advantage of Company Matches: If your employer offers a 401(k) match contribute at least enough to get the full match. It's essentially free money and by not taking advantage of it you're leaving money on the table.

4. Increase Contributions Over Time: As your income grows try to increase your retirement contributions. Even small increases can make a significant difference in the long run.

5. Catch-Up Contributions: If you're over 50 years old take advantage of catch-up contributions allowed by retirement plans. These additional contributions can help you make up for any lost time in building your retirement savings.

6.3 Identifying Investment Opportunities for Retirement Savings:

While saving for retirement is important it's equally important to invest your retirement savings wisely. Here are some investment opportunities to consider for your retirement portfolio:

1. Stock Market: Investing in individual stocks or stock market

index funds can provide potentially higher returns over the long term. However it's important to diversify your investments to reduce risk.

Example: Suppose you invested $10000 in a stock that delivered an average annual return of 10% over 30 years. Without reinvesting dividends your investment would grow to $76122. However with dividends reinvested it would grow to $237376.

2. Bonds: Bonds are debt instruments issued by governments or corporations. They can provide stable income in retirement and are considered less risky than stocks. However the returns are typically lower.

Example: If you invest $10000 in a bond with a 5% annual coupon rate you would receive $500 in interest income each year.

3. Real Estate: Investing in real estate such as rental properties or real estate investment trusts (REITs can provide both income and potential appreciation over time. This can diversify your retirement portfolio and provide stable cash flow.

Example: If you invest $100000 in a rental property with an expected annual rental income of $10000 and a 5% annual appreciation your total return after 30 years would be $609847.

4. Mutual Funds: Mutual funds pool money from multiple investors to invest in a diversified portfolio of stocks bonds or other assets. They offer professional management and diversification but come with associated fees.

Example: If you invest $10000 in a mutual fund that delivers an average annual return of 7% over 30 years your investment would grow to $76123.

Remember investing involves risk and it's important to consult with a financial advisor to determine the most suitable investment strategy based on your risk tolerance and retirement goals.

7

Paying Off Debt

Debt can quickly become a burden if not managed effectively. High-interest rates and fees can add up over time making it difficult to make progress in paying off debts. In this section we will explore strategies for managing and reducing debt prioritizing debt repayment methods for negotiating lower interest rates and tips for avoiding and managing credit card debt.

7.1 Strategies for Managing and Reducing Debt

Debt management requires a systematic approach to reduce and eventually eliminate your debts. Here are some strategies to consider:

1. Create a budget: Start by creating a comprehensive budget that includes all your income and expenses. This will help you understand how much money is available to allocate towards debt repayment.

2. Track your expenses: Keep track of your daily spending and identify areas where you can cut back. By reducing unnecessary expenses you can free up more money to put towards debt repayment.

3. Consolidate your debts: If you have multiple debts with high-interest rates consider consolidating them into a single loan with a lower interest rate. This simplifies your payments and can potentially save you money on interest.

4. Snowball method: This popular debt repayment strategy involves paying off your smallest debt first while making minimum payments on other debts. Once the smallest debt is paid off you can then focus on the next smallest debt. This method helps build momentum and motivation as you see smaller debts being eliminated.

5. Avalanche method: This method prioritizes paying off debts with the highest interest rates first. By focusing on high-interest debts you can save money on interest payments in the long run.

6. Increase your income: Find ways to increase your income such as taking on a second job or freelancing. The additional income can be used to accelerate debt repayment.

7. Negotiate with creditors: Consider reaching out to your creditors to negotiate lower interest rates or more favorable repayment terms. Some creditors may be willing to work with you to make your debt more manageable.

7.2 Prioritizing Debt Repayment

When prioritizing debt repayment it's crucial to have a clear understanding of your financial situation. Here's a common approach to prioritizing debts:

1. High-interest debt: Start by focusing on high-interest debts such as credit cards or payday loans. These debts typically have the highest interest rates and therefore paying them off first will save you the most money in the long run.

2. Secured debts: If you have any debts secured by collateral such as a car loan or mortgage it's important to prioritize these payments to avoid losing the asset. Falling behind on secured debts can lead to repossession or foreclosure.

3. Unsecured debts: Once you've tackled high-interest and secured debts you can move on to unsecured debts like personal loans or medical bills. While these debts may have lower interest rates it's still important to address them to improve your financial well-being.

By following a prioritization strategy you can focus your resources on the most impactful debts and gradually work your way towards financial freedom.

7.3 Methods for Negotiating Lower Interest Rates

Lowering interest rates can significantly reduce your debt burden. Consider these methods to negotiate lower interest rates with your creditors:

1. Contact your creditors: Reach out to your creditors and explain your financial situation. Ask if they can lower your interest rate waive fees or offer a more flexible repayment plan. Many creditors are willing to work with you to avoid default.

2. Utilize balance transfer offers: Some credit card companies offer promotional periods with low or zero interest rates for balance transfers. Transferring your high-interest debt to one of these cards can save you money on interest payments. However be mindful of any balance transfer fees and the duration of the promotional period.

3. Seek out debt consolidation loans: Consolidating multiple high-interest debts into a single loan with a lower interest rate can save you money on interest payments. Look for reputable lenders who offer debt consolidation loans and compare their terms and interest rates.

4. Consider credit counseling: Non-profit credit counseling agencies can provide guidance and assistance in negotiating lower interest rates with creditors. They can also help you create a personalized debt management plan.

Remember negotiation success depends on various factors such as your financial situation credit history and the goodwill of your creditors. It's essential to be persistent patient and polite when seeking lower interest rates.

7.4 Avoiding and Managing Credit Card Debt

Credit card debt is among the most common forms of debt that many people struggle with. To avoid falling into credit card debt and effectively manage existing ones consider the following tips:

1. Pay off your balance in full each month: Whenever possible pay your credit card balances in full by the due date. This helps you avoid paying any interest charges on your purchases.

2. Use credit cards responsibly: Avoid unnecessary purchases and use credit cards only for essential items. Practice restraint and avoid impulse buying as it can lead to excessive credit card debt.

3. Set a budget for credit card usage: Determine a limit on how much you can charge on your credit cards each month. Stick to this budget and resist the temptation to exceed it.

4. Pay more than the minimum payment: If you carry a balance on your credit card always pay more than the minimum payment. By doing so you can reduce the amount of interest you accrue over time.

5. Avoid cash advances: Cash advances on credit cards often come with high fees and interest rates. Whenever possible find alternative ways to access cash if needed.

6. Limit the number of credit cards you have: Owning multiple credit cards increases the risk of accumulating debt. Stick to a manageable number of cards and cancel or close unused ones.

7. Regularly review and monitor your credit card statements:

Keep a close eye on your credit card transactions to ensure they are accurate. Report any suspicious or unauthorized charges immediately.

It's crucial to be proactive in managing credit card debt to avoid falling into a cycle of accumulating high-interest debt. By following these tips you can make smarter financial choices and build a healthier financial future.

In conclusion paying off debt requires a combination of strategic planning disciplined budgeting and careful negotiation. Whether you're tackling credit card debt or other forms of debt the key is to be proactive persistent and patient. By implementing these money-saving tips you can gradually reduce your debt burden improve your financial well-being and work towards a more secure future.

8

Income-Boosting Strategies

8.1 Exploring Side Hustles and Part-time Jobs:

One effective way to boost your income and save more money is by taking on side hustles or part-time jobs. These additional sources of income can bring in extra money that can be used to increase your savings. Here are a few examples:

Freelancing: If you have a specific skill or talent such as writing graphic design web development or photography you can offer your services as a freelancer. Websites like Upwork Fiverr and Freelancer provide platforms to connect freelancers with clients looking for their skills. You can take on freelance projects during your free time allowing you to earn extra income without giving up your full-time job.

Delivery Services: Companies like Uber Eats DoorDash and Instacart offer opportunities for flexible part-time work. You can become a delivery driver and choose your own hours. This option is ideal for those who have a car and enjoy driving.

Tutoring or Teaching: If you have expertise in a particular field or are a certified teacher you can offer tutoring or teaching services. This can be done in person or online through platforms like VIPKid or Tutor.com. You can set your own rates and schedule making it a flexible and rewarding side hustle.

Renting Your Property: If you have an extra room in your house or an apartment that you don't use regularly you can consider renting it out on platforms like Airbnb. This can generate a significant amount of income especially if your property is in a desirable location.

Selling Handmade Products: If you are crafty and enjoy creating handmade items you can sell them on platforms like Etsy. This allows you to turn your hobby into a profitable venture. Whether it's homemade jewelry knitted goods or artwork there is a potential market for unique handmade products.

It's important to choose a side hustle or part-time job that aligns with your skills interests and available time. By leveraging these opportunities you can increase your income and save more money.

8.2 Advancing in Your Career for Higher Income:

Another approach to boosting your income and saving more money is by advancing in your career. Here are some strategies to consider:

Continuing Education: By investing in your education and acquiring new skills you can position yourself for higher-paying roles. This can involve taking courses attending workshops or pursuing advanced degrees. The more knowledge and expertise you have the more valuable you become in the job market increasing your earning potential.

Networking: Building a strong professional network can open doors to new opportunities. By attending industry events joining relevant associations and connecting with professionals in your field you increase your chances of finding higher-paying jobs or promotions. Many opportunities arise through personal connections and referrals so it's important to actively network and build relationships within your industry.

Seeking Promotions or Raises: Don't be afraid to advocate for yourself and seek promotions or raises in your current job. If you have been performing well and delivering value to your employer it's reasonable to ask for increased compensation. Prepare a case for why you deserve a promotion or raise highlighting your accomplishments and contributions. When negotiating be confident and articulate about your value to the company.

Exploring Job Market: Keep an eye on the job market to stay updated on industry trends salary ranges and in-demand skills. This information can help you understand your worth in the job market and negotiate better compensation packages. Additionally exploring job postings can help you identify higher-paying roles that may be a good fit for your skills and experience.

Taking on Leadership Roles: Volunteering for leadership positions within your organization or industry can demonstrate your skills and competence helping you stand out from your peers.

Leadership roles often come with increased responsibilities and higher compensation. By showcasing your leadership abilities you position yourself for higher-paying positions.

8.3 Utilizing Passive Income Streams:

Passive income streams are another effective way to boost your income and save more money without putting in extra hours of work. Passive income refers to money earned with minimal effort or ongoing involvement. Here are some examples:

Investing in Stock Market: Investing in the stock market can provide you with an opportunity to earn passive income through dividends and capital appreciation. By purchasing shares of companies and holding them for the long term you can benefit from regular dividend payments and potential stock price increases. It's important to conduct thorough research and consider your risk tolerance before investing in the stock market.

Rental Properties: Owning rental properties can be a lucrative source of passive income. By purchasing properties and renting them out to tenants you can generate a steady stream of rental income. However being a landlord comes with responsibilities such as property maintenance and managing tenants. It's important to carefully research the real estate market and understand the local rental laws before getting into property investment.

Peer-to-Peer Lending: Peer-to-peer lending platforms such as Prosper and LendingClub allow individuals to lend money to borrowers and earn interest on their investments. This provides an alternative to traditional banking systems and can generate a passive income stream.

Affiliate Marketing: If you have a blog website or social media following you can earn passive income through affiliate marketing. By promoting products or services and including affiliate links you can earn commissions when your audience makes a purchase through your link. This requires building an engaged audience and creating valuable content that drives sales.

Digital Products: Creating and selling digital products such as e-books online courses or software can be a profitable passive income stream. Once you have created the product you can sell it repeatedly without investing additional time or effort. Platforms like Teachable and Gumroad make it easy to create and sell digital products.

It's important to note that while passive income streams can be lucrative they often require initial investments of time or money. Additionally some passive income streams come with risk and may require ongoing management. Therefore it's crucial to do thorough research and evaluate the feasibility and potential returns before diving into passive income ventures.

By exploring side hustles advancing in your career and utilizing passive income streams you can boost your income and save more money. Implementing these strategies requires dedication discipline and careful planning. Remember to set clear financial goals track your progress and make adjustments as necessary. With time and consistent effort you can achieve financial stability and build a brighter future.

9

Smart Shopping Techniques

9.1 Comparing Prices and Utilizing Price-tracking Tools:

One of the most basic yet effective ways to save money while shopping is to compare prices. Before making a purchase take the time to research different retailers and websites to find the best deals. With the rise of e-commerce it has become easier than ever to compare prices across multiple platforms.

For example let's say you're in the market for a new laptop. Instead of settling for the first option you come across you can visit various online retailers such as Amazon Best Buy and Walmart to compare prices. By doing so you might find that the same laptop is available at a significantly lower price on a different website.

Alongside manually comparing prices you can also utilize price-tracking tools to help you save money. These tools monitor the prices of products across different retailers and notify you when there is a price drop or a better deal available. Some popular price-tracking tools include Honey Camelcamelcamel and PriceAlert.

For instance let's say you have your eye on a particular pair of shoes. You can add them to your watchlist on a price-tracking tool and it will notify you when there is a price reduction or a better deal available. This way you can ensure that you buy the product at the lowest possible price and make the most of your money-saving efforts.

9.2 Couponing and Cashback Opportunities:

Another money-saving technique is utilizing coupons and cashback opportunities. Coupons are a great way to save money at the checkout counter. You can find coupons in newspapers magazines and online couponing websites. Additionally many retailers offer their own coupons or have coupon codes available on their websites.

Let's say you're planning to go grocery shopping. By clipping coupons from your local newspaper or printing them out from online sources you can save a significant amount on your grocery bill. It's important to check for expiration dates and any specific terms and conditions associated with the coupons to ensure your savings are valid.

Cashback opportunities allow you to earn money back on your purchases. Many credit cards offer cashback rewards programs where you earn a percentage of your spending as cashback. Additionally there are websites and apps like Rakuten (formerly known as Ebates) and Swagbucks that offer cashback on online purchases. By using these platforms you can earn money while shopping.

For example suppose you use a credit card with a 2% cashback reward program and spend $500 on groceries each month. By the end of the year you would have earned $120 in cashback. This is an additional saving that can be used towards future purchases or to pay off your credit card bill.

9.3 Saving on Online Shopping and Avoiding Impulse Purchases:

Online shopping has become incredibly popular and it offers several opportunities to save money if you approach it strategically. Here are some tips for saving money when shopping online:

a) Use Promo Codes and Discounts: Before checking out always search for promo codes or discounts. Many online retailers offer special promotional codes that can be applied during the checkout process providing you with discounts or free shipping. Websites like RetailMeNot and Coupons.com are great resources for finding available discount codes.

b) Take Advantage of Free Shipping: Shipping costs can add up so look for online retailers that offer free shipping or have minimum order thresholds to qualify for free delivery. If you're buying from multiple retailers consider consolidating your purchases into one order to reach the minimum threshold and avoid paying extra for shipping.

c) Utilize Customer Reviews: Prior to making an online purchase it's beneficial to read customer reviews. These reviews provide valuable insights into the quality and performance of the product from people who have already purchased it. By doing so you can avoid wasting money on subpar products and make more informed buying decisions.

d) Avoid Impulse Purchases: Online shopping can be tempting especially when there are flash sales limited-time offers or attractive deals. However impulse purchases can quickly drain your savings. To avoid falling into this trap create a shopping list and stick to it. Take the time to consider whether you really need the product and if it aligns with your budget and long-term goals.

For example let's say you come across a limited-time sale for a TV that seems like a steal. Instead of immediately making the purchase take a step back and evaluate if it fits within your budget and if you genuinely need a new TV. By avoiding impulsive buying decisions you can save yourself from regret and potential financial strain.

Conclusion:

Smart shopping techniques such as comparing prices utilizing price-tracking tools couponing cashback opportunities and applying strategies for online shopping can help you save a significant amount of money. By being proactive and diligent in your shopping habits you can make the most of your hard-earned money while still enjoying the things you need and want. Remember each penny saved adds up over time contributing to your overall financial well-being.

10

Long-Term Financial Planning

Long-term financial planning is essential for achieving financial stability and security over an extended period of time. It involves strategies and actions aimed at building wealth managing risks and protecting assets for the future. In this article we will explore three crucial aspects of long-term financial planning: building an emergency fund investing for future financial security and estate planning and asset protection all of which can help individuals and families save money.

10.1 Building an Emergency Fund:

Building an emergency fund is an important aspect of long-term financial planning. An emergency fund is a designated amount of money set aside to cover unexpected expenses or financial emergencies such as medical bills car repairs or job loss. It acts as a safety net and helps individuals avoid going into debt or using credit cards to deal with unforeseen circumstances.

Here are some practical tips for building an emergency fund:

1. Determine the size of your emergency fund: Financial experts recommend saving three to six months' worth of living expenses in your emergency fund. Calculate your average monthly expenses and set a target amount accordingly.

2. Pay yourself first: Treat your emergency fund as a priority expense and contribute to it regularly. Set up automatic transfers from your paycheck or checking account to ensure consistent savings.

3. Cut unnecessary expenses: Look for ways to trim your budget and redirect those savings towards your emergency fund. Cancel unused subscriptions or memberships reduce dining out or minimize impulse purchases.

4. Increase your income: Consider exploring additional sources of income such as freelancing or part-time work to boost your savings. All the extra money earned can go directly into your emergency fund.

5. Keep the fund liquid: It's important to keep your emergency fund in a liquid and easily accessible account. A high-yield savings account or a money market account can be great options which offer both safety and potential growth.

Example: Jane is a working professional earning $60000 per year. After analyzing her expenses she determines that her monthly living expenses are approximately $3000. To meet the recommended three to six months' emergency fund target Jane aims to save $9000 to $18000. She creates a monthly budget and begins contributing $500 to her emergency fund each month until she reaches her goal.

10.2 Investing for Future Financial Security:

Investing is a key component of long-term financial planning for building wealth and securing a comfortable retirement. By investing wisely individuals can potentially earn higher returns than traditional savings accounts and beat inflation. Here are some money-saving tips for investing:

1. Start early: The power of compounding allows investments to grow over time. The earlier you start investing the more time your investments have to grow potentially leading to greater wealth accumulation.

2. Diversify your portfolio: Diversification is essential for reducing risk. Spread your investments across different asset classes like stocks bonds and real estate as well as different industries and regions.

3. Take advantage of tax-efficient accounts: Maximize contributions to tax-advantaged retirement accounts like 401(k)s or IRAs. These accounts offer tax benefits such as tax-deferred growth or tax-free withdrawals during retirement.

4. Invest based on your risk tolerance: Understand your risk tolerance and invest accordingly. Balancing higher-risk investments with more conservative ones can help manage risk and ensure a stable investment portfolio.

5. Keep investment costs low: Pay attention to fees associated with investment products. Look for low-cost index funds or exchange-traded funds (ETFs) with low expense ratios to minimize investment costs.

6. Stay informed and review your investments: Regularly review your investments and stay updated with market trends and news. Consider seeking professional financial advice to make informed investment decisions.

Example: John a 25-year-old professional starts investing $200 per month in a low-cost index fund that historically generates an average return of 8% annually. Assuming John continues investing for the next 40 years and earns an average annual return of 8 his investment of $200 per month would grow to approximately $473000 by the time he reaches 65.

10.3 Estate Planning and Asset Protection:

Estate planning is often overlooked but plays a crucial role in long-term financial planning. It involves the process of organizing and arranging one's affairs to ensure that assets are protected and distributed according to one's wishes in the event of incapacity or death. Here are some essential considerations for estate planning and asset protection:

1. Create a will or trust: A will outlines how your assets should be distributed after your passing while a trust can provide more control and flexibility in managing your estate. Both allow you to determine beneficiaries and minimize probate costs.

2. Review and update beneficiaries: Regularly review and update beneficiary designations on your retirement accounts life insurance policies and other assets to ensure they align with your wishes and goals.

3. Consider life insurance: Life insurance can provide financial protection for your loved ones in the event of your premature death. Evaluate your insurance needs and consider term life insurance or permanent policies based on your circumstances.

4. Plan for incapacity: Establish durable powers of attorney for healthcare and financial matters to designate trusted individuals who can make decisions on your behalf if you become

incapacitated.

5. Protect your assets: Explore strategies to protect your assets from potential lawsuits or creditors. Depending on your situation this could involve creating trusts setting up limited liability companies (LLCs or using exemptions allowed by law.

6. Seek professional guidance: Estate planning can be complex and it's advisable to consult with an estate planning attorney or financial advisor who specializes in this area. They can help navigate legal requirements tax implications and ensure your plan reflects your unique circumstances and goals.

Example: Sarah a 40-year-old homeowner and parent consults an estate planning attorney to create a comprehensive estate plan. With the help of the attorney she establishes a revocable living trust to avoid probate designates guardians for her children updates her beneficiaries on retirement accounts and life insurance policies and considers setting up a family limited liability company (LLC) to protect her investment properties.

In conclusion long-term financial planning is crucial for individuals and families aiming for financial stability and security. Building an emergency fund investing for future financial security and estate planning are key components of such planning. By following these money-saving tips and taking appropriate actions individuals can ensure they are prepared to handle emergencies grow their wealth and protect their assets in the long run. Remember financial planning is a continuous process that requires discipline regular review and adjustment based on changing circumstances.

11

Money Saving Tips

1. Create a monthly budget and stick to it.
2. Cut down on eating out and cook meals at home.
3. Use coupons and look for deals when shopping.
4. Buy generic brands instead of name brands.
5. Cancel unnecessary subscriptions and memberships.
6. Use public transportation or carpool instead of driving alone.
7. Reduce energy consumption by turning off lights and appliances when not in use.
8. Bundle your home and auto insurance for savings.
9. Shop around for the best prices on insurance policies.
10. Cancel cable or satellite TV and switch to streaming services.
11. Lower your cellphone bill by choosing a cheaper plan or switching providers.
12. Buy used items instead of new whenever possible.
13. Grow your own vegetables and herbs in a garden.
14. Cancel unused gym memberships and exercise at home or outdoors.

15. Plan meals ahead and avoid impulse grocery shopping.//
16. Buy in bulk for items you use frequently.
17. Take advantage of cashback or reward programs.
18. Shop at thrift stores for clothing and household items.
19. Lower your water bill by fixing any leaks and using water-efficient fixtures.
20. Use a programmable thermostat to save on heating and cooling costs.
21. DIY home repairs and maintenance when possible.
22. Use reusable shopping bags instead of buying plastic ones.
23. Cut back on expensive beauty and grooming products.
24. Find free or low-cost entertainment options such as parks libraries and community events.
25. Sell unused items or have a yard sale to make extra money.
26. Use public libraries for books magazines and movies instead of buying them.
27. Save money on gas by combining errands and planning efficient routes.
28. Cancel unnecessary home services such as landscaping or house cleaning.
29. Compare prices and get quotes from multiple vendors before making big purchases.
30. Set up automatic savings transfers to a separate account.
31. Use a water filter instead of buying bottled water.
32. DIY gifts instead of buying expensive ones.
33. Cut back on alcohol consumption to save money.
34. Avoid impulse purchases and wait 24 hours before buying non-essential items.
35. Bring your own lunch to work instead of buying meals.
36. Use online resources or free tutorials for DIY projects instead of hiring professionals.

37. Negotiate lower interest rates on credit cards or loans.

38. Take advantage of free or discounted events in your community.

39. Lower your internet bill by negotiating with your provider or switching plans.

40. Maintain a good credit score to qualify for lower interest rates.

41. Use a clothesline instead of a dryer when weather permits.

42. Buy gift cards at a discount or use discounted gift cards for purchases.

43. Plan vacations during off-peak seasons for better deals.

44. Cancel unused or underused bank accounts to avoid fees.

45. Use online comparison sites to find the best deals on flights hotels and rental cars.

46. Cut down on alcohol consumption when dining out to save money.

47. Avoid ATM fees by using your bank's ATMs or getting cash back at stores.

48. Avoid impulse purchases by waiting 30 days before buying non-essential items.

49. Cancel unnecessary streaming subscriptions and share accounts with family or friends.

50. Use a water-saving showerhead and faucet aerators to reduce water usage.

51. Buy refurbished electronics instead of new ones.

52. Take advantage of free trials for services or products before committing to a subscription.

53. Use a programmable thermostat or smart home technology to regulate temperature and save on energy costs.

54. Brew your own coffee at home instead of buying it from coffee shops.

55. Cut back on non-essential beauty and grooming services.

56. Use public Wi-Fi instead of using cellular data when possible.

57. Cancel unnecessary credit cards to avoid annual fees.

58. Lower your car insurance premium by increasing your deductible.

59. Plan your grocery shopping around sales and discounts.

60. Use a price comparison app or website when shopping online.

61. Repair or repurpose items instead of buying new ones.

62. Take advantage of free educational resources online instead of paying for courses.

63. Avoid paying for unnecessary extended warranties.

64. Cut down on energy usage by unplugging electronics when not in use.

65. Cancel unused magazine or newspaper subscriptions.

66. Buy seasonal produce when it's cheaper and more readily available.

67. Use a water-saving toilet or install a dual-flush system to reduce water consumption.

68. Reduce food waste by planning meals and using leftovers creatively.

69. Use ceiling fans instead of running the air conditioning all the time.

70. Buy items in the offseason when they are on sale or clearance.

71. Cancel unused streaming services or share subscriptions with family or friends.

72. Use home remedies or generic medications instead of expensive branded options.

73. Cut down on impulse purchases by practicing the 30-day

rule.

74. Shop at discount or thrift stores for clothing and household items.

75. Use a clothesline or drying rack instead of using a dryer for laundry.

76. Cancel unused or unnecessary magazine and newspaper subscriptions.

77. Use energy-efficient light bulbs and turn off lights when not needed.

78. Buy in bulk for items you use frequently to save money.

79. Brew your own coffee at home instead of buying it from a coffee shop.

80. Buy generic brands instead of name brands when shopping.

81. Eat out less frequently and cook meals at home to save money.

82. Use public transportation or carpool instead of driving alone.

83. Cancel unnecessary subscriptions and memberships.

84. Lower your energy consumption by turning off lights and appliances when not in use.

85. Negotiate lower interest rates on credit cards or loans.

86. Shop around for the best prices on insurance policies.

87. Cancel cable or satellite TV and switch to streaming services.

88. Lower your cellphone bill by choosing a cheaper plan or switching providers.

89. Buy used items instead of new whenever possible.

90. Grow your own vegetables and herbs in a garden.

91. Cancel unused gym memberships and exercise at home or outdoors.

92. Plan meals ahead and avoid impulse grocery shopping.

93. Take advantage of cashback or reward programs.

94. Shop at thrift stores for clothing and household items.

95. Lower your water bill by fixing any leaks and using water-efficient fixtures.

96. Use a programmable thermostat to save on heating and cooling costs.

97. DIY home repairs and maintenance when possible.

98. Use reusable shopping bags instead of buying plastic ones.

99. Cut back on expensive beauty and grooming products.

100. Find free or low-cost entertainment options such as parks libraries and community events.

www.ingramcontent.com/pod-product-compliance
Lightning Source LLC
LaVergne TN
LVHW020437080526
838202LV00055B/5230